Dewi Sant
Saint David
Patron of Wales

J. B. Midgley

GRACEWING

First published in 2012

Gracewing
2 Southern Avenue,
Leominster
Herefordshire HR6 0QF
www.gracewing.co.uk

ISBN 978 085244 758 1

Front cover: Design for the mosaic of St David in Westminster Cathedral by Ivor Davies, photograph appleskruffz@aol.com.

Back cover: Detail of the mosaic executed by Tessa Hunkin, haloes by Killian Shermann, photograph courtesy Westminster Cathedral.

Dewi Sant

Saint David

In pia memoria
E. de T. W. L
R. I. P

'They must be servants in my sanctuary, responsible for guarding the Temple gates and serving the Temple' (Ezekiel 44:11).

CONTENTS

FOREWORD

The Most Reverend Peter D. Smith
Archbishop of Southwark

Given at
Saint David's Cathedral
Charles Street
Cardiff

Few contemporary records survive of the life of Saint David, the Patron Saint of Wales, yet Barry Midgley has drawn up a very well researched and fascinating account of the life and influence of this great Celtic Saint. It is set in the context of the developing Celtic spirituality in the fifth and sixth centuries strongly influenced by monastic tradition. It is a story of extraordinary faith and courage in preaching the Gospel in the very difficult circumstances of the Barbarian invasions and the collapse of civil authority. It is a story of ecclesiastic reform, of loyalty to the one Church of Christ and a commitment to orthodox teaching lived out day by day in a life of vibrant faith and hope, of personal discipline and self-sacrifice.

One of the great achievements of Saint David and his monks was to recall careless Christians to a fervent life and to revitalize faith and commitment to the Gospel. His parting words were; 'Persevere in those things that you have learned from me. Be joyful and keep the Faith.' That is a message that is as relevant today as it was in the days of Saint David. It has never been easy to live the Christian life; it demands a deep faith, a profound hope and an unconditional love which reaches out especially to the poor, the needy and the rejected. Saint David's life shows us that it can be done cheerfully and to the great benefit of the society in which we live.

Saint David's example should be an inspiration to all of us who try day by day to follow in the footsteps of Our Lord and Master Jesus Christ. Through his intercession may we, like him, remain ever faithful to the gift of faith which we share with this great Welsh Saint.

✠ Peter, Archbishop of Southwark

The author records his gratitude to Archbishop Peter for his great kindness in writing the foreword while Archbishop of Cardiff, and before his translation to Southwark on 19th June 2010.

1

PATRON SAINTS

Christians honour the men and women of the Church Triumphant and acknowledge their sanctity that illuminate the path of their pilgrimage to God though His Son, Jesus Christ. The Blessed Virgin Mary and the Saints are holy because their lives conform to that of Our Lord, demonstrate the inherent values of the Gospel, and offer a model for the Christian life. In those days when the Church was severely persecuted, special homage was paid to the martyrs who suffered to the point of death, and the homage paid to them united Christians in a common memory and devotional practice that invoked their intercession. When the Peace of Constantine brought the age of persecution to an end, the reverential cult of martyrs was extended beyond 'red martyrdom' of shedding one's blood to 'white martyrdom'. This was the crown of those who severed themselves from the mainstream of worldly life by becoming ascetics and monks in lonely places, who suffered imprisonment or ill-usage for the Faith, or who fulfilled all the obligations of life, often described as 'the fearsome daily round,' with heroic and persevering fortitude. So that there is no misunderstanding, the Church reminds us that only God is worshipped, and the prayers offered, and the honour paid to the Blessed Virgin Mary and the Saints in private and public devotions enrich the worship that is due to God through Christ in the Holy Spirit.

As individuals, members of occupation groups, dioceses, and countries, we are moved to adopt particular Saints as our venerated protectors, guardians and intercessors whose memory we cherish, and on who we feel can be called upon for help in finding solutions to a variety of problems. In a special way, they also intercede for us to Our Lord for the forgiveness of offences, give support in those times of temptation when the Devil makes assaults on souls, encourage good deeds, and offer comfort in times of distress and misfortune. By way of popular devotion and not necessarily by official designation or appointment, they may become patrons of countries with whose history they have been associated, of professions in which they were engaged, or of recognised needs in which they exercised a healing ministry. Of particular comfort is the watchful care of personal patrons whose names have been received in Baptism, or when the religious life is embraced. The relevant associations of patronage may sometimes be difficult to identify, but the Holy Spirit ensures that all well-intentioned devotion is made holy and valid and, therefore, the Saints always respond to the prayers that are directed to Heaven.

Even though the Feasts of some may no longer be listed in the Roman Calendar that was revised in 1969 in the wake of the Second Vatican Council, travellers need not think that their confidence in Saint Christopher is misplaced. Those looking for a taxi can still remember Saint Fiacre who was adopted as patron of hackney carriages, in French called 'fiacres' because their cab-stand was at the hotel Saint-Fiacre in Paris. Those needing a dentist might call upon Saint Apollonia who, in the first stage of her martyrdom, is said to have been tortured by having her teeth withdrawn by pincers, and promised to help those suffering from toothache.

Patriotism and Nationhood

In the context of a country's Patron Saint, the Fathers of the Second Vatican Council, 1962–1965, remind Christians that it is entirely proper to develop a loyal devotion to their country, but they must remain concerned for

> the welfare of the entire human family that is united by the bonds that link races, peoples and nations. Christians who are gathered together in the Church of all nations live for God and Christ by following the honourable customs of their own nation. As good citizens they practice true and effective patriotism and foster a universal love for humanity without racial prejudice or hypernationalism.[1]

Later, Pope John Paul II explained that the responsibility of patriotism, (the English word coming from the late Latin *patriote* which derived from the Greek *patrios* 'of one's fathers'), is included in the Fourth Commandment to honour one's parents who represent God the Creator when He gives us life. Through them is acquired the spiritual patrimony of one's native land that calls for the duty of *pietas*, the religious dimension of the veneration to which mothers and fathers are entitled. Patriotism is a love for everything that is to do with that land: its history, traditions, language, natural features, and the accomplishments of compatriots.[2] It understands that the common good of citizens involves accepting the responsibility to serve the continuing development of society, and recognizes that, even in an age of changing international structures, the native land is a permanent reality in which the natural societies of family and nation are not mere conventions but part of human nature's social dimension. Pope John Paul II admonishes us to be wary of allowing our patriotism to develop into an unhealthy nationalism. Though a society's cultural and historical identity is preserved within the concept of nation, (Latin *natus*, 'born'), its function must not degenerate into a nationalism that is preoccupied only with the good of one's own nation.

> The cultural and historical identity of any society is preserved and nourished by all that is contained within this concept of nation. Clearly, one thing must be avoided at all costs: the risk of allowing the essential function of the nation to lead to an unhealthy nationalism... Whereas nationalism involves recognizing and pursuing the good of one's own nation alone, without regard for the rights of others, patriotism, on the other hand, is a love for one's native land that accords rights to all other nations equal to those claimed for one's own. Patriotism, in other words, leads to a properly ordered social love.[3]

The Church reminds us that fallen humanity is prone to belligerent tendencies. Nearly a century ago, when Pope Benedict XV wrote to the nations that were involved in the First World War, he pointed out that to prevent war and achieve peace, armaments should be reduced by international agreement, material force be replaced by moral right, and disputes be resolved by arbitration. He warned that exaggerated nationalism and militarist assumptions that wars are inevitable are obstacles to peace in the world.[4] This theme was continued by Pope Pius XI in his *Peace Letter to the World* of Christmas 1922. There he wrote that to prevent the moral and material destruction of civilization and to ensure world peace, the love of peace must be deeply rooted in our hearts. The true peace of Christ can only exist in the Kingdom of Christ.[5]

Saint David, Patron of Wales in Europe, was endowed with remarkable qualities as a spiritual leader who brought the Gospel to the Celtic tribes, and his dedicated response to the call of Christ to take the Gospel to all nations is a continuing example for modern evangelists. In the first Encyclical of his Pontificate, Pope Benedict XVI wrote that, in His kindness, God provides every age with holy men and women to support His People, and the Holy Spirit breathes an impetus to refresh faith, religious leadership, and energy in the mission that Christ delegates to His Church. The lives of the saints are not limited to their earthly biographies but also include their being and working in God after death. In the saints one thing becomes clear: those who draw near to God do not withdraw from men, but rather become truly close to them.[6]

On 1st March, the Feast of Saint David, the Church prays:

God our Father,
you gave the Bishop David to the Welsh Church
to uphold the Faith
and to be an example of Christian perfection.
You made him a pastor of your Church
to feed your sheep with his word
and teach them by his example.
In this changing world
may he help us to hold fast to the values
which bring eternal life.

Notes

[1]   Vatican II, *Ad gentes*, 15.

[2]   See Pope John Paul II, *Memory and Identity: Conversations at the Dawn of a Millennium* (New York: Rizzoli, 2005), pp. 65–66.

[3]   *Ibid.*, p. 67.

[4]   See Pope Benedict XV, *Note to the Heads of Belligerent Peoples* (1 August 1917), calling for an end to the First World War in *AAS* 9 (1917), pp. 417–420. While First World War was raging, the Pope had the courage to call it a 'senseless slaughter'. See also Pope Benedict XVI in his *Angelus Message* at Lorenzago di Cadore (Belluno) on 22nd July 2007, in which he referred to the *Note* of his predecessor Pope Benedict XV.

[5]   Cf. Pope Pius XI, Encyclical Letter *Ubi arcano Dei consilio*, 49.

[6]   See Pope Benedict XVI, *Deus Caritas est* (2005), 18, 40.

2

EVANGELISATION IN EUROPE

In the Sermon on the Mount, Our Lord and Redeemer proposes a series of qualities, attitudes, and values which please God without necessarily including financial success, achievement, power, or popularity.

> How blessed are the poor in spirit: the kingdom of Heaven is theirs.
> Blessed are the gentle: they shall have the earth as inheritance.
> Blessed are those who mourn: they shall be comforted.
> Blessed are those who hunger and thirst for uprightness: they shall have their fill.
> Blessed are the merciful: they shall have mercy shown them.
> Blessed are the pure in heart: they shall see God.
> Blessed are the peacemakers: they shall be recognised as children of God.

> Blessed are those who are persecuted in the
> cause of uprightness: the kingdom of Heaven
> is theirs.
> Blessed are you when people abuse you and
> persecute you and speak all kinds of calumny
> against you falsely on my account.
> Rejoice and be glad, for your reward will be
> great in heaven (Mt 5: 3–12).

In these Beatitudes, God the Son reveals the goal of
human existence, the ultimate end of human activity
as God the Father invites us to His own Beatitude in
God the Holy Spirit. This calling is addressed to each
individual and to the whole Church, 'the new people
who have accepted the promise of the Blessed Trinity,
who draw life from it by their faith, and accept the
privilege of passing it to others, evangelised so that
they may evangelise'.[1] To conclude the Beatitudes, Our
Lord makes a warm, personal address that underlines
the importance of Christian discipleship:

> You are the salt of the earth. But if salt becomes
> tasteless, what can make it salty again? It is
> good for nothing, and can only be thrown out
> to be trampled underfoot. You are the light of
> the world. A city built on a hill-top cannot be
> hidden. No one lights a lamp to put it under a
> tub; they put it on the lamp-stand where it
> shines for everyone in the house. In the same
> way, your light must shine in the sight of
> everyone so that, seeing your good works, they
> may give praise to your Father in Heaven (Mt
> 5: 13–16).

The world, the 'earth', depends for its well-being on
the preservative influence of His followers. and, as His
audience was well aware, when preserving salt

becomes insipid, nothing can be done to restore its flavour, and it is good for nothing but to be thrown into the rubbish bin, just as the disciple who loses fervour is ignored by the world. The comparison changes to light which, like salt, is a necessity of life. In a world of darkness, disciples have a social obligation to light the way to the Father by their humble example. If we shirk this responsibility, then we fail in our duty, and will be as much use as a lamp hidden behind the flour-bin: 'For there is nothing hidden but it must be disclosed, nothing secret except to be brought to light' (Mt 5:1–16; Mk 4:21–25).

Our Lord has awakened memories of Isaiah's warning: 'Share your bread with the hungry, and shelter the homeless poor, clothe the man you see naked and do not neglect your own flesh and blood. Then will your light shine like the dawn and your wound quickly be healed' (Is 58:7–10). St John Chrysostom comments:

> Let us not overlook Him here, hungry, in order that He Himself may feed us there. Here let us clothe Him, that He may not send us forth naked from the safe refuge with Him. If we give Him to drink here, we shall not say with the rich man: 'Send Lazarus to dip the tip of his finger in water and cool our tongues' (Lk 16:24). If here we receive Him into our homes, there He will prepare many mansions for us. If we go to Him when He is in prison, He Himself will free us also from our bonds. If, when He is a stranger, we take Him in, He will not look down upon us as strangers when we are in the Kingdom of heaven, but will give to us a share in the heavenly City. If we visit Him when He is sick, He Himself will quickly free us also from our infirmities.[2]

Saint Francis of Assisi entreats us: 'Preach the Gospel wherever you go. Even use words if necessary.'

Jesus knew that the proclamation of the Gospel was the centre of His ministry: 'I must proclaim the Good News of the Kingdom of God to the other towns too, because that is what I was sent to do,' and He delegated this same mission to His Apostles. 'Go out to the whole world: proclaim the Good News to all creation.' Before ascending to His Father, his final words were, 'All authority in heaven and on earth has been given to me. Go, therefore, make disciples of all the nations; baptise then in the name of the Father and of the Son and of the Holy Spirit, and teach them to observe all the commands I gave you.' His authority is constant and He assures them, 'Know that I am with you always; yes, to the end of time' (Lk 4:43; Mk 16:15; Mt 28:18–20).

In her turn, the Church inherits Our Lord's mandate through the Apostles and makes the words of Saint Paul her own—'Not that I boast of preaching the Gospel, since it is a duty which has been laid on me; I should be punished if I did not preach it' (1 Co 9:16).

Consequently, she sends her missionaries to the four corners of the earth until such time as infant churches are fully established and can continue their own work of evangelisation. By proclaiming the Gospel, she 'prepares hearers to receive and profess the Faith, disposes them for Baptism, releases them from the slavery of error, and incorporates them into Christ so that, through charity, they may grow to full maturity in Him'.[3] The purpose of mission is 'evangelization and the planting of the Church where it has not yet taken root', a responsibility not only of bishops and clergy but of all Christ's disciples according to their ability. The universal Church is missionary and proclaiming the Gospel is the basic duty of the People of God.[4]

The Fathers of the Second Vatican Council recognised that the first means of evangelising is the witness of Christian life on the part of the Church and its members. The Church both prays and labours in order that the entire world may become the People of God, the Body of the Lord and the Temple of the Holy Spirit, and that in Christ, the Head of all, all honour and glory may be rendered to the Creator and Father of the Universe.[5] Christ, becoming obedient even unto death and because of this exalted by the Father, entered into the glory of His kingdom. To Him all things are made subject until He subjects Himself and all created things to the Father that God may be all in all. Now Christ has communicated this royal power to His disciples that they might be constituted in royal freedom and that by true penance and a holy life they might conquer the reign of sin in themselves. Further, He has shared this power so that serving Christ in their fellow men they might by humility and patience lead their brethren to that King for whom to serve is to reign. But the Lord wishes to spread His kingdom also by means of the laity, namely, a kingdom of truth and life, a kingdom of holiness and grace, a kingdom of justice, love and peace.[6]

The mission of the Church is fulfilled by that activity which makes her, obeying the command of Christ and influenced by the grace and love of the Holy Spirit, fully present to all men or nations, in order that, by the example of her life and by her preaching, by the sacraments and other means of grace, she may lead them to the faith, the freedom and the peace of Christ;

that thus there may lie open before them a firm and free road to full participation in the mystery of Christ.[7]

On the Feast of Our Lady's Immaculate Conception, 1975, Pope Paul VI published his Apostolic Exhortation *On Proclaiming the Gospel in the Modern World*. This document, *Evangelii Nuntiandi*, regarded by many commentators as his most significant pronouncement, was inspired by the culmination of that Holy Year which coincided with the tenth anniversary of the conclusion of the Second Vatican Council, and the Third General Assembly of the Synod of Bishops which focused on evangelisation. The Pope linked the process of evangelisation with the abiding concern of the Church to proclaim the coming of God's reign as liberation from sin and the Evil One, and from economic, social, and political oppression. He concluded that the essence of the Church's mission is to evangelise, and she begins by being evangelised herself.[8]

As the third millennium dawned, the late Pope John Paul II reminded the world that it could not live by bread alone, and so the Church must be able to give convincing witness to the words which Jesus Christ spoke.[9] Jesus Christ is the one and only Mediator of salvation for all of humanity. Only in Him do humanity, history and the cosmos find their definitively positive meaning and receive their full realization: He has in Himself, in His Life and in His Person, the definitive reason of salvation. He is not only the Mediator of salvation but salvation's very source.[10] The Pope continued:

> The Church, as the bearer of the Gospel, thus helped to spread and consolidate those values which have made European culture universal. With all this in mind, the Church of today, with

a renewed sense of responsibility, is conscious
of the urgency of not squandering this precious
patrimony and of helping Europe to build herself
by revitalizing her original Christian roots.[11]

Cardinal Cormac Murphy-O'Connor, then Archbishop
of Westminster, called for a confident commitment to
tell the world about the Kingdom of God, and recommended meditation upon 'the Gospel's relevance in
the daily tasks of life in a deep relationship with Christ
who teaches us in parables.' The report of the Bishops'
Conference, *Evangelisation in England and Wales*, that
appeared in 2002, reiterated the Pope's recognition of
a time and opportunity when Christians must proclaim the Gospel with renewed confidence, conscious
of their Baptismal call to continue the Apostolic
mission to make disciples of all nations in the name of
the Holy Trinity. It recommended a refreshed evangelism that begins with a personal affirmation of faith
nurtured by continued religious education, prayer,
and scripture-study groups in the parish community.
At Your Word Lord, a renewal programme for the
Westminster diocese, was followed by the establishment of the Agency for Evangelisation, with a
reminder that evangelisation is the grace and vocation
of the Church, and that learning about the Faith
continues throughout life.

Contemporary circumstances of evangelisation on
the Continent of Europe may not be as physically
hazardous as those encountered by heroic ancestors
in faith like Saint David but they are no less urgent,
especially in a society experiencing radical change.

In September 2004, senior Catholic Bishops from the
member States met in Council to discuss the European
Constitution, the need to strengthen international

ecumenism to help preserve Christianity, and the
co-ordination of efforts to re-evangelise Europe. Pope
John Paul II sent a message urging them to guide their
people, 'to rediscover their common spiritual roots and
the enduring wisdom of their Christian heritage.' He
reminded Christendom that the history of the Church
continues to evolve, that Christ is the centre of the
universe, and that 'openness to the world' does not
demand a secularisation of Catholic theology nor
adaptation of Faith to conform to a 'post-Christian
culture'. He counselled a balanced judgement which
recognises that enthusiasm for 'change' does not
necessarily ensure 'progress'. It must not obscure that
which is of Faith, nor reject what has stood the test of
time and remains relevant to such good effect. In July
2010, his successor Pope Benedict XVI announced the
establishment of a major new Vatican agency for the
re-evangelisation of Europe to stimulate Christianity's
revival and counter widening, counter-productive
secularisation. The Holy Father's initiative has been
welcomed by the Archbishop of Westminster, and the
Bishop of Arundel and Brighton, who has responsibility for evangelisation in England and Wales, observed
that the Church must attend to its primary mission of
proclaiming the Gospel with tolerance, welcome and
compassion.[12]

The man responsible for leading Pope Benedict's
mission to re-evangelize traditionally Christian countries, Archbishop Salvatore (Rino) Fisichella, is predict-
ing that October 2012 will be the most important
month to date for the Church's New Evangelization.
Bishops from around the world will convene in Rome
to discuss the New Evangelization at a synod—just as
Pope Benedict XVI launches his *Year of Faith*. Arch-

bishop Fisichella has said 'The mission of the new evangelization, is to announce that Jesus Christ is the true answer to all the questions that men and woman have today trying to make sense of our lives.'[13]

It is unfortunate that the European Constitution makes no acknowledgement of Christianity's historic contribution to the development of European civilisation and political life. Christian pioneers in Europe and beyond have demonstrated that Divine Law enriches life and enhances liberty. They shaped cultural development by way of artistic and intellectual inspiration, preserved and reproduced classical literature to advance learning, and pioneered progress in architecture, agriculture, and engineering. They introduced systems of justice, social order, health, education, and promoted the inalienable right and dignity of the individual who is best supported by the social pillars of marriage, parenthood and family life. Their adaptation of Roman Law created a model for contemporary legislation that is available to society as it contemplates the future and learns how to preserve what is of lasting value. They helped engender stable attitudes that have exercised a beneficent global influence upon civil and administrative justice that enables other states to place the welfare of citizens before other considerations. Whatever the deficiencies of their Christian successors, from their early efforts can be traced the concepts of democracy, liberty and tolerance that prompt host nations to offer sanctuary.

Far beyond his patronage of Wales, Saint David is a European hero who is still eager to help us with his powerful intercession.

Notes

1   *Catechism of the Catholic Church*, 1719.
2   St John Chrysostom, *Homily 25 on St John's Gospel*, 3.
3   Vatican II, *Lumen gentium*, 17.
4   Cf. Vatican II, *Ad gentes*, 6, 35.
5   Vatican II, *Lumen gentium*, 17.
6   Vatican II, *Lumen gentium*, 36.
7   Cf. Vatican II, *Ad gentes*, 5.
8   Cf. Pope Paul VI, Apostolic Exhortation *Evangelii Nuntiandi*, 9, 12, 15, 18, 29, 40–48.
9   Pope John Paul II, Post-Synodal Apostolic Exhortation *Ecclesia in Europa*, 69.
10 See *ibid.*, 20. See also Synod of Bishops, Second Special Assembly for Europe, *Instrumentum Laboris*, 30.
11 Pope John Paul II, *Ecclesia in Europa*, 25.
12 See *Catholic Herald* (9 July 2010).
13 Archbishop Rino Fisichella, as quoted by *Catholic News Agency* (22 November 2011).

3

CELTIC SPIRITUALITY

A consideration of Celtic religious and social life awakens renewed appreciation of Saint David's dedication and monumental contribution to the history of Christianity.

Nearly a century before his birth, Rome and its Empire had become a focus for barbarian attacks and annexation so that, in 410 AD, the Emperor Honorius found it necessary to withdraw from Britain the Roman garrisons that by now included many Christians. With the departure of the competent military force, northern German tribes like the Angles and Saxons of Schleswig Holstein and the Jutes of the Rhineland sensed an opportunity to take possession of a land on which they had long cast envious eyes, and identified areas for conquest in East Anglia, Essex, Sussex, Wessex, Kent and Hampshire.

The Britons did not succumb easily to invasion and mounted valiant resistance for more than a century, but the disappearance of Roman military presence, law, order, and initiative had severe repercussions. Also seriously affected was the early infrastructure of the Church that had enjoyed the support of the Roman See of Peter, contact with which was now extremely difficult. Saint Gildas Bandonicus (500–570), originally from the Clyde in Scotland was an eminent monk at Llaniltud in South Wales and an influential figure in Welsh monastic life especially through his writings. In his book, *The Desolation of Britain*, he reflected sadly on the result of the Saxon invaders:

> In this way were all the settlements brought low with the frequent shocks of the battering rams; the inhabitants, along with the bishops of the church, both priests and people, whilst swords gleamed on every side and flames crackled, were together mown down to the ground, and, sad sight! there were seen in the midst of streets, the bottom stones of towers with tall beam cast down, and of high walls, sacred altars, fragments of bodies covered with clots, as if coagulated, of red blood, in confusion as in a kind of horrible wine press.[1]

This work, cited by Saint Bede the Venerable in his *History of the English Church and People*, reveals the decadence that had infected British rulers and clergy and attributes the success of the Angles and Saxons to the infidelity of these leaders. Gildas records that many conscientious laity and clergy migrated to Cumbria, Cornwall, Brittany, and to Wales where the monastic houses that had already been founded by intrepid Celtic monks offered a haven where the Faith could be practised in comparative safety.

   Monastic life had found its genesis in the East, especially Egypt, and the lives of the Desert Fathers fired the imagination of the Christian world. The great Saint Athanasius was familiar with the monastic customs that had evolved and, when he wrote his *Life of Saint Antony of Egypt*, the pioneering abbot of monastic solitude and asceticism, it was welcomed with enthusiasm in the West.[2] During the fifth century, monasticism spread rapidly from Egypt to Gaul and thence to Wales, Cornwall and Ireland, and became the influential and beneficent element in both the Church and society, especially in lands where clans and tribes were more important as social units than towns and cities. The response of these populations was so positive that when a king or chief embraced Christianity he often became a monk and built a monastery. Monastic 'towns' thus developed as mixed settlements of men, women, married couples, children, and celibates that fulfilled social, economic and education functions, and conducted the teaching of the Faith with spiritual care. Not surprisingly, the organisation of the Church tended to be more monastic than diocesan, and where the king or chieftain was a monk, he would undertake the duties of a Father Abbot. By the middle of the fifth century, many large monasteries flourished in Western Britain, so much so that five hundred or so instances of a 'Llan' are to be found on modern maps of Wales. The word originally meant 'enclosure', but was later used to indicate a 'church' and testified to the remarkable fidelity of the Welsh to resurgent Christianity fifteen centuries ago.

Celtic spirituality focused upon the religious development of the individual, whether monastic or lay, and introduced the practice of guidance known as 'soul friendship'. The essential role of religion in the everyday life of the people became evident in a profound sense of God's encompassing presence and, because the Celts were geographically dependent on both the land and the sea, their prayers and poetry are rich in powerful natural imagery. Their spirituality appreciated the solitude and asceticism of the Desert Fathers that was now often practised in remote islands and headlands, and the wanderings of individuals and groups led them, sometimes unintentionally, to evangelise the peoples they encountered and among whom they settled.

The monasticism of the Celts was austere and involved physical penance and fasting but, despite the rigours that might have sapped mental energy, culture flourished. It is seen in the artistic achievement of Celtic illustrations, decorative illumination of manuscripts and metalwork that are masterpieces of art-history, and the writings that reveal assiduous study and scholarship. In a spirit of self-denial, the monks accepted *peregrinatio pro Christo*, that is the travelling exile undertaken on behalf of Christ, and with extraordinary faith and courage they took the Gospel to Scotland, the Channel Islands, Brittany, and Western Europe. The journeys of Saints like Brannoc, Brelade, and Barry involved crossing dangerous waters in tiny boats and coracles, but they were undeterred by scant navigational experience, or uncertainty as to what they would encounter if land were ever reached. The speed and skill with which they established monastic colonies in the cause of evangelisation defies human explanation and must surely have been heaven-blessed.

Ninian, Samson, Illtyd and Paulinus

It is not surprising that Celtic monasticism won great renown for its salutary influence on Welsh life as it imbued a sense of national identity that dispelled disconcerting feelings of vulnerability and stemmed the flow of emigration to Cornwall and Brittany. In addition to Saint Gildas whom we have already met, the great and saintly abbots whose fame was not confined to their own land, included Ninian, Samson, Illtyd and Paulinus. Ninian from North Wales was a remarkable scholar, and tireless travelling preacher who evangelised the Picts in Forfar, Perth and Stirling. According to Saint Bede, 'they accepted the true Faith through the preaching of Bishop Ninian, a most reverend and holy man of the British race who had been instructed in the mysteries of the Christian Faith in Rome.'[3]

Saint Samson is hailed as the most important Welsh missionary of the sixth century. Assisted by his compatriots and disciples Saints Austell, Mewan and Winnoc, he worked in Cornwall and Dorset where he founded the Abbey of Milton Abbas, and his Apostolic activity also took him to Brittany, the Scilly Isles where one bears his name, and Guernsey where a town is called after him. His Feastday of 28th July appeared in the National Calendar until its revision in 1969. Illtyd, a disciple of Saint Germanus, was praised by Saint Samson 'as the most learned Briton in the study of the Scriptures and Philosophy.' He founded the Abbey of Llantwit Major, the most influential in South Wales that housed hundreds of monks.

Paulinus, friend of Illtyd and another pupil of Saint Germanus, is sometimes remembered as Saint Pol after the region of Paul just south of Newlyn in Cornwall where he won fame as an evangelising Bishop, and from where he conducted a mission in Brittany where he was much revered as a 'peregrinus pro Christo'. He is credited with the foundation of Llangors in Breconshire where there is still a Llan 'Beulin', and there are further memorials to him at Capel Beulin and Ffynnon ('Well') Beulin. A stone discovered in the Carmarthenshire parish of Caeo and dated not later than the mid-sixth century is thought to mark his burial place. It bears a Latin inscription that in translation reads, 'Preserver of the Faith, and ever a lover of his country; here Paul lies, most devout fosterer of goodness.' He is gratefully remembered for inspiring and nurturing the achievements of Saint David who was destined to become head of the Welsh Church, and whose active influence was to achieve pre-eminence at a time when the pagan Saxons were still intent on overwhelming Christians. Dafydd Sant would be acknowledged as Patron of Wales from the twelfth century.

The Pelagian Heresy

Saint Ninian was a redoubtable opponent of his compatriot, the heretic monk Pelagius (360–420), who taught that humanity was capable of arriving at faith and achieving salvation by its own efforts, and did not therefore need the help of God's grace. He left Britain to circulate his teaching in Rome where he attracted a great many followers, some of whom he sent back to win more adherents, and their success after his death alarmed loyal British bishops. They felt they needed help and so appealed to Pope Saint Celestine I who, as Peter's successor, had claimed authority over the Church in both East and West. Accordingly, in 429, he sent to Britain Saint Germanus of Auxerre who did not consider himself as coming from a separate community, but rather as a fellow Bishop in the universal Catholic Church. Assisted by Saint Lulus of Troyes, Germanus assembled a conference at Verulanium, the scene of Saint Alban's heroic witness, where he demolished the Pelagian position though he found it necessary to return fifteen years later when the heresy revived.[4] The request for help and the effective response show how the Church in Britain, Rome and Gaul was united in Faith. Germanus, whose authority emanated from the Pope's directive, was revered by British Christians and his honoured memory reflects the loyalty of the British Church to Rome and Saint Peter.

Saint Patrick and Menevia

In Pembrokeshire there is a beautiful coastal vale that was known as the *Vallis Rosina* or Glyn Rhosyn, and it nestles in an area once called Mynyw, a name Latinised first to Menapia then to Menevia. Even before David was born, and as we shall learn from what is known of his early education, it was a religious centre which Saint Patrick, yet another disciple of Saint Germanus, visited before going to Ireland in 432 AD. Rhygyfarch says he so loved the *Vallis Rosina* that he decided that this was the place where he would devote himself to the service of God. He began by opening a monastic school that was known as Ty Gwyn, the White House, where Saint Non was probably educated, and which later developed as a seminary college for Irish missionaries.

However, Providence had other plans for Patrick. An angel of the Lord came to him as he slept and told him that God had not disposed this place for him but for a son not yet born, nor would he be born until thirty years had passed; this is a reference to Patrick's inspired prophesy of David's birth.[5] He was then favoured with a vision of Ireland, the country where he was to be God's chosen Apostle: 'Rejoice Patrick, for the Lord has sent me to show you the whole of Ireland from the seat which is in Vallis Rosina.'[6] Sure enough, Saint Patrick's Chapel in Porth Mawr marks his departure point for Ireland whose mountains can be seen from Eisteddfa ('Seat') Badrig, and it was in his beloved *Vallis Rosina* that David, whose birth he had announced, would locate the monastery church that one day would be St David's Cathedral.

Further indicators of Patrick's sojourn in Menevia are Capel Padrig in Naverne, Pembrokeshire, and Patter Dock with Patter's Church that is now Pembroke Dock.[7] There is a place near Tenby that is called after Saint Issel who was one of Patrick's lesser known companions and collaborators. His name is also preserved at Killishea in Ireland which, in happy exchange, later adopted David as its patron. In further reciprocation, there are churches dedicated to Saint David in the Irish dioceses of Cloyne, Ferns and Kildare and, the church of Clonard in County Meath possesses a stained glass window that portrays him teaching Saint Finnian who would become the eminent Abbot of Clonard and one of the 'Twelve Apostles of Ireland'.

The *Catalogue of the Saints of Ireland* that was written in the eighth century offers the information that 'they received the Mass from Bishop David, Gildas and Doccus'.[8] Of course, the Mass was already known, celebrated and loved in Ireland but, because the Welsh Saints were geographically closer to Rome and Gaul, they probably became aware of liturgical details and reforms sooner than their Irish brethren to whom they could then transmit them. This would have been natural given the close, friendly relationship between the Irish and Welsh monks. Today, the Catholic church of Saint David and Saint Patrick in Haverfordwest, that was founded in the diocese of Menevia in 1872, preserves the memory of this joyous association. Doccus mentioned above was also called Drocco and, more particularly, Saint Congar. He came from Pembrokeshire, and was one of the Welsh missionaries who founded Christian communities in Devon and Somerset where at Congresbury, from Congar, his relics, mentioned in mediaeval pilgrim guides, were enshrined. In former times, Wales and the South West celebrated his feast on 27th November.

Notes

1   St Gildas, *De Excidio Britanniae* (The Ruin of Britain), 24.

2   St Athanasius, *Vita Sancti Antonii* in *PG* 26, 835–978.

3   St Bede, *Ecclesiastical History of England*, Book III, chapter 4.

4   Verulanium was an ancient town in Roman Britain, situated to the southwest of the modern city of St Albans in Hertfordshire. A large portion of the Roman city remains unexcavated, being now park and agricultural land, though much has been built upon. The ancient Watling Street passed through the city.

5   Rhygyfarch, *Life of St David*, 3.

6   *Ibid*.

7   See S. Baring-Gould & J. Fisher, *The Lives of the British Saints. The Saints of Wales and Cornwall and such Irish Saints as have Dedications in Britain* IV (London: The Honourable Society of Cymmrodorion, 1913), pp. 60, 71.

8   D. N. Dumville et al, Saint Patrick. A. D. 493–1993 (Woodbridge: The Boydell Press, 1999), p. 140.

4

Saint David

The Written Life of Saint David (Dafydd, Dewi)

David is first mentioned briefly in the tenth century manuscript *Annales Cambriae*, Cambria being an earlier name of Wales. However, his chief biographer is Rhygyfarch (in Latin *Ricemarchus*) who was the son of Julian, Bishop of the diocese of St. David's in Pembrokeshire, a relationship which need not come as a surprise given that it predated the Church's universal requirement of clerical celibacy. Rhygyfarch became a monk at Llanbadarn, Aberystwyth, where in 1090 he wrote his *Buchedd Davi* (*The Life of David*) that is the main source of available knowledge. Though the biography contains many edifying stories, it would be a mistake to dismiss it as nothing more, and the author points to his reliance on 'old documents in the archives of St. David's Cathedral that include some by the Saint himself.' In 1923, Rhygyfarch's work was edited by the Anglican scholar A. W. Wade who said of him that 'he revealed the instincts of the historian' though, as Thomas Carlyle pointed out, 'history can be a distillation of rumour'.[1] In this regard it is possible that Bishop Julian had persuaded his son to emphasise the independence of the bishops and the Church in Wales. William the Conqueror enjoyed the support of Pope Alexander II and, not long after his success at Hastings and acquiring the English throne, won his approval to appoint two outstanding Archbishops, first Lanfranc in 1070 and then Saint Anselm in 1093. His intention was that all Britain would ultimately submit to the jurisdiction of 'Augustine's See of Canterbury', hence Bishop Julian's intent.

Birth and Parentage

There was something of a competitive spirit among the mediaeval biographers of the Saints though, in fairness, their enthusiastic eulogies were motivated by a genuine devotion and an acceptance of the manifestations of God's presence and power in human history. Rhygyfarch was no exception in ensuring that his Saint David was not be surpassed in wonder and miracle. He began by telling that Saint Patrick was inspired by an angel to prophesy David's birth thirty years before the event.[2] This took place in 497 AD at Henvynyw that is identified as the site of the former Roman garrison of Loventium in what is now Cardiganshire.

David's father was Sant, a prince of the line of Cunedda, who is sometimes called Sandda or Xanthus, all three names meaning 'saint'. Sant's own father Ceredig gave his name to Cardiganshire, and his mother was the daughter of Brychan from whom Breconshire originates. Sant had been told in a dream that his son would be blessed with three gifts: a stag to reflect his lordship over the Serpent who deceived our First Parents in the Garden of Eden, a fish to indicate his life-long abstinence from meat, and a swarm of bees whose honey would be sweet testament to his holiness.[3]

> These gifts foretell his life, for the honeycomb proclaims his wisdom, for as honey lies in wax, so he held a spiritual mind in a temporal body. And the fish declares his aquatic life, for as a fish lives in water, so he, rejecting wine and beer and everything that can intoxicate, led a blessed life in God on bread and water only. The stag signifies his power over the Old Serpent, for as a stag, having deprived serpents of their food, seeks a fountain of water and is refreshed as in youth with the strength received, so he, borne on high as on stags' feet, deprived the Old Serpent of the human race of his power of hurting him and fled to the fountain of life with constant flowings of tears, and, being renewed from day to day, so brought it to pass that in the name of the Holy Trinity, by the frugality of moderate repasts, he began to have saving knowledge and the power of governing demons.[4]

Some believed that Sant was a nephew of King Arthur but, in the twelfth century, Geoffrey of Monmouth was more of the opinion that Arthur was a nephew of David who may not therefore have been an only child. Despite Sant's name, there is no evidence that he was particularly holy, although some say that 'Lezant' near Launceston in Cornwall may be so called to honour his memory.

There are no doubts about the sanctity of David's mother Saint Non, or Nonnita, who was the daughter of Gynyr of Caergawch, a Pembrokeshire chieftain.

She gave birth to her illustrious son during some
unusually stormy weather in a place now commemo-
rated by the ruined Chapel of Saint Non. David was
baptised by Saint Ailbe who wrote a monastic Rule,
was famed as a travelling evangelist and founder-
Bishop of the Tipperary diocese of Imlech in the
province of Munster, 'and was led by Divine Providence from Ireland to Henvynyw at this time'. Not
only did a miraculous spring of water suddenly appear
to facilitate the administration of the Sacrament, but
an elderly monk who had been blind from birth 'took
some of the water in which the infant David had been
thrice dipped, and sprinkled it thrice on his own face,
whereupon he received sight for the first time.'[5]

After the death of her husband Sant, David's mother
Non became a nun 'renowned for her holiness, and as
the spiritual mother of many religious women'. She
founded a convent at Altarnum, south of Launceston
on what is now the A30 road, where some of her relics
came to rest in a chapel and a well was built in her
honour. There are two dedications to Saint Non in
Pelynt, not far inland from Polperro, two more in
North Wales, one in Bradstone, Devon, and her name
lives on in five Welsh parishes. Another 'Saint Non's
Well', on the coast about two miles west of where St
David's Cathedral now stands, is a fine example of the
healing holy well that figures prominently in Celtic
faith. Early civilizations needed water for their settlements and the Celts revered the pure water that these
wells provided as a sacred gift from God.

Saint Non's missionary activity extended to Ireland
and finally to Brittany. There she has a beautiful tomb
and effigy at Dirinin where a mystery play used to be
performed annually in her loving memory. She is still

revered by Bretons who attribute the authorship of a *Life of Saint David and Saint Non* to the Crusading King Richard the Lionheart of England. Her feast in the Roman Martyrology was on 3rd March, though William of Worcester pointed out that it was celebrated in Altarnum and Launceston on 25th June and 3rd July respectively.

Notes

1   T. Carlyle, *The French Revolution. A History* (1837), Pt. I, Bk. VII, ch. 4.

2   Rhygyfarch, *Life of St David*, 3.

3   *Ibid.*, 2.

4   *Ibid.*

5   *Ibid.*, 7. See also L. Toke, 'St. David' in *The Catholic Encyclopedia* (New York: Robert Appleton Company, 1908). Retrieved 26 January 2012 from *New Advent*: http://www.newadvent.org/cathen/04640b.htm.

5

David, Monk and Reformer

Early Education

At Henvynyw, 'the holy David walked to school every day to learn the alphabet, the Psalms, the lessons for the whole year, and the Masses.' We do not know to whom Sant and Non entrusted their son's early education but, given the details of the above syllabus, one can reasonably surmise that, thanks to Saint Patrick, there were still monks in the area who provided tuition for the children. Later, David embraced the monastic life and studied for the Priesthood at Ty Gwyn, Saint Patrick's 'White House' Seminary, under the benign direction of Saint Illtyd (Illtud).[1]

After his ordination, David went to Whitland in Carmarthenshire where he studied the Scriptures for ten years with academic guidance from Illtyd and Paulinus. It did not take Paulinus long to recognise that David possessed outstanding qualities, and he nominated him to be his eventual successor as Abbot of Whitland. However, having been so informed in an angelic visitation, he told him that he must first undertake a mission of evangelisation. In a spirit of obedience, David prepared by immersing himself in a period of solitary prayer in the Vale of Ewias, where Llantony Abbey was later built. He then set out to take the Gospel to other territories some of which were alien or hostile, occasionally on horseback, often on foot, and always with a total disregard for distance, hardship and danger. He proclaimed the Good News of the Kingdom of God and was successful in recruiting to the religious life many generous souls who would teach and demonstrate the life of Faith that has been handed down from the Apostles. Rhygyfarch provided a map of David's itinerary, and from this it looks as if he established or reformed twelve religious foundations that included Glastonbury, Bath, Croyland, Repton, Leominster and Raglan. If this were not enough, he is credited as founding fifty parish churches throughout Wales which joyfully carry his name to this day. Meanwhile, Saint Paulinus lived to the great age of one hundred and four but, in his later years became afflicted with blindness, which David is reported as having 'cured by his prayers and making the Sign of the Cross over his beloved master'.[2]

The English monk and historian William of Malmesbury (1080–1143), tells us that the foundation of Glastonbury Abbey pre-dated the arrival of David who intended only a conditional dedication and to donate a portable altar that was adorned with a great sapphire. Our Lord favoured him with vision to tell him that He Himself had already dedicated Glastonbury in honour of His Mother, and that a re-dedication was therefore not necessary. Accordingly, David commissioned only an extension the dimensions of which

William recorded (and these were archaeologically verified in 1921). Inevitably, the sapphire altar would have been confiscated by Henry VIII at the time of the Dissolution of the Monasteries, and it is possible that this stone may now be among the Crown Jewels.

According to tradition, when David went to Bath to establish a monastery, 'he there caused deadly water to become healthy with a blessing, and endowed it with a salutary heat, rendering it fit for people to bathe'.[3] However, the chronicler may have forgotten that the Romans, in their desire to introduce Britons to restorative public bathing in *Aqua Sulis*, had anticipated this miracle by a couple of centuries!

The reference to the 'twelve monasteries' founded by David may be so numbered as symbolic of the 'sacred twelves' in Israel's history such as the twelve tribes, or, by association, the twelve Welsh tribes he is said to have converted or, most significantly, the Twelve Apostles. It is also possible that the number is an historical emulation of the twelve monasteries founded by Saint Benedict mentioned by Pope Saint Gregory the Great in his biography of Europe's Patron. Admittedly, Rhygyfarch and others depended to some extent on local traditions that escape firm historical confirmation, but there is little doubt that David did establish monastic settlements and numerous churches ('Llans') in neighbouring regions that had previously been pagan and even unfriendly.[4]

The Reformer

Having returned from his apostolic journeys, Abbot David built his principal monastery on the Ty Gwyn site in the Vallis Rosina of Menevia, and placed it under the protective patronage of Saint Andrew the

Apostle and Patron of Scotland. Andrew's cult was very popular in the West not least in Anglo-Saxon Britain where Cynewulf's Old English poem 'Andreas' celebrated his journeys including the one to Scotland where he landed at St Andrew's, and his Feast on 30th November was already universal by the sixth century. The long and fruitful relationship between the Celtic monks may have further influenced David's choice of name for his monastery that would become St David's only after his death. There is some conjecture that he might have inherited the site and buildings from his father Sant who, perhaps, was one of those well-disposed and convert rulers or leaders who founded monastic settlements for their subjects, and even served as abbots. In addition to Saint Andrew's patronage, the monastery became familiarly known as Ty-Dewi, 'David's House', and the entire area as Dewsland or 'Dewi's Land'.

Like all Celtic monks, David and his community rigorously observed the austere rule and ascetic practices of the Desert Fathers that had been adopted in Gaul and transmitted to Britain. They fashioned their own habits from animal skins, and followed a demanding schedule of manual labour that required pulling the plough themselves without the help of oxen. They drank only water, certainly never beer, abstained from meat, and ate only bread with salt, herbs, watercress and, maybe, the occasional leek. Saint Benedict's experiences at Subiaco were replicated when maidservants, at the behest of the resentful wife of a local chieftain called Boia, made obscene and futile attempts to seduce the monks of Ty-Dewi.[5] Then, as happened in Benedict's case, some of David's community who recoiled from his demanding standards poisoned his bread, and he was saved only by the timely arrival from Ireland of Saint Scuthyn who alerted him to the deadly loaf which he blessed and ate himself without any ill effects.[6]

The monks' life of prayer included fidelity to the Divine Office, evenings spent in meditation, reading and writing, and the observance of a strict vigil of prayer from Friday evening to Sunday morning with only one hour's rest after midnight on Saturday. They were devoted to evangelical poverty, and declined any personal possessions to the extent that they would never lay claim for example to 'my book,' but only to its use for which they had permission. David himself earned the epithet *Aquaticus* (The Waterman) a reference perhaps to the number of baptisms he conducted, or the only drink that ever passed his lips, or his favourite penance of totally immersing himself in cold water while reciting the Psalms that he loved as the prayers of his Lord Jesus.[7] He took to heart Saint Paul's recommendation to Saint Timothy that became a prevailing tenor of the charisma with which he encouraged his brethren and wider flock. 'As one dedicated to God, you must aim to be saintly and religious, filled with faith and love, patient and gentle. Fight the good fight of the Faith, and win for yourself the eternal life to which you were called when you made your profession and spoke up for the truth in front of many witnesses, following Jesus who spoke up for the truth in front of Pontius Pilate' (1Tm 6:11–13).

In a confused world Celtic monasteries like David's beacons of stability and purpose. For his part, David won universal acclaim for his selfless devotion to works of charity and mercy, and his manifest, personal holiness and pious practice that included frequent genuflections to remind himself and others of God's abiding presence. Gerald of Wales, writing in the twelfth century, applauded him as 'the great ornament and example of his age who formed many pastors and servants of God.'

In addition to evangelising and instructing the people, the monastic orders increasingly disseminated the arts of music, painting, architecture, carving and sculpture. They copied books, wrote and embellished manuscripts, and opened libraries. They built schools, hospitals, dormitories, kitchens, dairies, butteries, bakeries, laundries, and guest houses where they extended hospitality as though they were greeting Christ Himself. They developed systems of farming and land management, and used water-pipes, filter-tanks and drains in the construction of lavatories, washing troughs, and the bath-houses they provided for the sick and infirm. As their international character grew, monasteries became communication channels of news, and temporal rulers and their subjects appreciated the wise advice of monks who were trained in regular habits of routine, business, accountancy and, above all, who were motivated by the ideals of service to the people.

David later made significant missionary journeys to Ireland, Brittany and Cornwall, and in these endeavours his faithful companions were Saints Teilo and Padern, otherwise called Paternus of Wales. Teilo, who was from Penally in Pembrokeshire, had been a loyal assistant to both Saints Samson and Paul Aurelian and, in due time, would be elevated to the Bishopric of Llandaff where his body rests today in the Cathedral. Padern was to found the Abbey of Llanbadarn Fawr in Dyfed from where, as Abbot and Bishop, he evangelised the neighbouring areas. With them, David also went on pilgrimage to Rome and Jerusalem. They found it wonderful that, from earliest days, pilgrims undertake devout journeys to places made holy by the presence of Our Lord, Our Lady, and the tombs of the Saints. Their pilgrimage becomes an interior journey of self-discovery as they become convinced of the presence of God who responds to their prayer for spiritual and physical help, and as they do penance for their offences and thank Him for His goodness in granting favours already received.

On the occasion of their journey to Jerusalem, the three saintly pilgrims had reached Gaul when 'an Angel endowed Father David with the gift of tongues just like the Apostolic gathering of old, so that he was able to communicate with and inspire those who lived in that country.' The Patriarch and highest ranking Bishop of Jerusalem was prepared for their arrival because he, too, had been favoured with a visit from an Angel. The heavenly messenger told him that 'three Catholic men are coming from the limits of the West. You are to receive them with joy and the grace of hospitality, and consecrate them to the episcopate.'[8] With great joy, the Patriarch duly anointed David as Archbishop, and Teilo and Padern as Bishops:

> When it was time for them to return home, he presented David with four gifts: a consecrated altar, a remarkable bell, a crozier, and a vestment woven with gold. To save them being burdened with such impediments on their journey home, he sent them to Wales by way of angels.[9]

The Synods

Archbishop David had not long returned from Jerusalem with Bishops Teilo and Padern when the Synod of Brevi in Cardiganshire was convened in by Saint Dyfrig, the Archbishop of Caerleon-on-Usk. Originally from Madley near Hereford, he was also known as Dubricius or Devereux and had also been a disciple of Saint Germanus. Dyfrig's intention was to quell some further interest in the heresy of Pelagius that had arisen, but the impressive assembly of bishops, abbots, monks, princes, delegated clergy and eminent laity did not make much progress until Saint Paulinus suggested that David should take charge as the Synod's President. Despite his humble misgivings and protests, he accepted the responsibility in obedience and duly won great approval for his eloquence and positive approach to ensuring the efficiency of the Synod's decision-making process.

Because this ecclesiastical council was held in the open air, some of those at the back of the assembly found it difficult to see David let alone hear him. When they drew attention to this, 'the ground on which he stood rose miraculously as he was preaching so that standing on this hill he might be seen and heard by all, lifting his voice like a trumpet, and a white dove settled on his shoulder, a sign of God's approving grace and blessing.'[10] Some less credulous commentators have pointed out that, given the geographical features in this part of Wales, any such miracle would have been superfluous. It is a pious and edifying story, but it is more likely that the ever practical David simply asked all the participants to join him on the hilltop. The village of Llandewi Brefi, 'David's church at the River Brevi' marks the Synod's location.

Rhygyfarch reports that David's consecration as Archbishop by the Patriarch of Jerusalem was warmly welcomed at the Synod and confirmed by popular acclaim:

> He had made such an impression that, with the consent of all the Bishops, Kings, princes, nobles, and all grades of the entire Britannic race, he was made Archbishop, and his monastery, too, is declared the metropolis, the principle church, of the whole country, so that whoever ruled it would be accounted Archbishop.[11]

At first, David's sense of unworthiness prompted him to decline the appointment but, again, obedience to God's will prevailed over his humility. Writing fifty years after Rhygyfarch, Gerald of Wales says that, 'He proved to be a vigorous and dedicated pastor, a guide to the religious, a light to the poor, a support to orphans, a father to the fatherless, a rule to monks, and a path to the laity.' In his ministry to all, he kept in mind the words of Saint James: 'The wisdom that comes from above is essentially something pure; it also makes for peace, and is kindly and considerate, full of compassion and shows itself by doing good' (Jm 3:16–18).

Bernard, the first Norman bishop of St David's, echoed Gerald's claim that David's appointment and metropolitan status was more than justified. However, it is unlikely that David and his successors would have enjoyed the type of Archiepiscopal and Metropolitan authority that carried responsibility for associated dioceses as it is understood today. Abbots in the Celtic Church were often consecrated bishops, but this did not mean that they were invested with diocesan responsibility in the canonical sense. It is probable, therefore, that David's was one of the monastery-bishoprics that coincided with the period of a particular Abbot's tenure. Nevertheless, even if the title of Archbishop may have been honorary, it was certainly an indication of popular, personal pre-eminence, and such was the regard in which David was held.

It is a measure of his authority, influence and acceptability that David took it upon himself to convene the Synod of Victory at Caerleon-on Usk in order to erase the remaining vestiges of Pelagianism once and for all.

> A crowd of bishops, priests and Abbots renewed what they had confirmed in the former Synod of Brevi, some useful matters being added. So, from these two synods, all the churches of our country take their standard and rule by Roman authority. The decrees which he had confirmed with his mouth, the Bishop David alone committed to writing with his own sacred hand, to be confirmed later by the Pope, Saint Felix IV, who had opposed the heresy with great determination.[12]

Gerald of Wales notes that 'David's writings were treasured in his Cathedral before the attacks of pirates laid waste to the Welsh maritime provinces.'

According to the *Book of Llandav*, when the time was right, Saint Dyfrig resigned from his See in David's favour and 'gave him the title of metropolitan Archbishop of Wales.' David then transferred the Seat of ecclesiastical government to Menevia where the future St David's became the Cathedral city of the Western See. According to Geoffrey of Monmouth who, it must be said, was not always reliable, it was Dyfrig who crowned Arthur King of Britain. Perhaps this explains why Alfred, Lord Tennyson in his poems 'The Idylls of the King' honoured him as 'high saint and chief of the Church in Britain':

> And holy Dubric (Dyfrig) spread his hands and
> spake
> 'Reign ye, and live and love, and make the world
> Other, and may the Queen be one with thee,
> And all this Order of thy Table Round
> Fulfil the boundless purpose of their King.'[13]

The Good and Faithful Servant

David's efforts on behalf of God's People in Wales and beyond continued unabated and, despite the relentless physical demands with no diminution in his asceticism, he lived to a ripe old age. Received wisdom has it that 1st March 589 is the most probable date when he entered into the joy of the Lord whom he had served so valiantly. There is also an opinion that the year might have been 604. If this were the case, one might hope David had the joy of knowing that Saint Gregory the Great, who had been elected Pope in 590, had commissioned the conversion of England through Saint Augustine and his monks who arrived in 597. However, though his support would have been unequivocal, he might not have been too enthusiastic about the less ascetic monasticism of the Italian Benedictines.

At Mass on the Sunday prior to March 1st, David preached a particularly inspiring sermon to the large congregation, but he began to feel unwell shortly after the Consecration. When the celebration of Mass had been completed, he blessed the people with his customary warmth and asked them 'to persevere in what you have learned from me and what you have seen with me. On 1st March I shall go the way of my fathers. Farewell in the Lord; never shall we be seen on this earth again.' As 1st March dawned, an angel comforted him with the news that 'the long desired day is at hand', and with great happiness and contentment he replied, 'Lord, let your servant now depart in peace.'[14]

His last words to his sorrowing community were 'Be joyful, and keep your faith and your creed. Do the little things in life that you have seen me do and what you have heard about. I am going to walk the path that our fathers have trod before us.' The chronicler adds that 'the monastery was filled with angels as Christ received his soul'.[15] David's exhortation 'Do the little things in life' became the well-loved and inspirational Welsh 'Gwnewch y pethau bychain mewn bywd.'

In the presence of a multitude of grieving mourners representing every level of society who came from far and wide, David was buried with great solemnity in his Cathedral-church of Saint Andrew. The position of his shrine was to be moved first in 1131, and again in 1275 by Bishop Richard Carew of St David's who had been able to modify, extend, and embellish the building thanks to the generosity of visiting pilgrims. John of Glastonbury, writing at the end of the twelfth century, claimed that in the reign of King Edgar in the year of Christ 963, the relics of Saint David were transferred to Glastonbury Abbey, though this is highly unlikely unless it refers only to a portion of the relics. John may have been gently inviting Welsh pilgrims who crossed the Bristol Channel on their to the Canterbury shrine of Saint Thomas Becket, martyred there in 1170, to make a detour to Glastonbury. Be that as it may, there was certainly great devotion to

David in Glastonbury that honoured him as one of its patrons.

It was shortly after David's death that the title of his monastery was changed from St Andrew's to St David's, an indication of his elevation to the company of the Saints by popular accord. Its acclaim as a centre of ecclesiastical reform, discipline and orthodoxy continued to grow and, when King Alfred the Great, despite his preoccupation with warding off the Danish invaders, wished to open his first school in the kingdom of Wessex, he asked Asser, a monk of St David's, to become its head. Asser, who had achieved great renown for his work and ministry, was reluctant to abandon all his current responsibilities but obediently agreed to divide his time between the Court and Menevia. He later became the distinguished Bishop of Sherborne, Alfred's biographer, and an energetic promoter of devotion to Saint David in Wessex. He died in 909.

Notes

1 See *The life of St Illtud* probably composed in Cemis, Pembrokeshire, in the twelfth century. Found in the British Museum Cotton MS Vespasian, A xiv.

2 See Rhygyfarch, *Life of St David*, 11.

3 *Ibid.*, 13.

4 *Ibid.*

5 See *ibid.*, 17.

6 *Ibid.*, 37–38.

7 See T. D. Griffen, Address to the Saint David's Society of Saint Louis, 'Saint David Aquaticus' (3 March 1996), pp. 2–3.

8 Rhygyfarch, *Life of St David*, 46.

9 *Ibid.*, 48.

10   *Ibid.*, 52.

11   *Ibid.*, 53.

12   See *ibid.*, 55.

13   Lord Alfred Tennyson, *Idylls of the King*.

14   See Rhygyfarch, *Life of St David*, 59.

15   *Ibid.*, 63.

6

CANONISATION AND CULT

There is no evidence that the great Saints of the early centuries like Patrick and David were officially canonised by Rome. Veneration of a person as a Saint by popular acclaim and local custom could be sanctioned and regulated by the diocesan bishop, and the 'cult' or homage was therefore local. Other bishops could, of course, grant permission for such veneration to be practised in their dioceses and, as it became more widespread, Rome might grant either tacit or explicit approval. When Callistus II succeeded to the Throne of Peter in 1119, he made it his first Papal responsibility to preside at the Council of Reims. Delegates to the Council included the aforementioned Bishop Bernard of St David's who, with a brother bishop, seized the opportunity to discuss with the Holy See matters related to Welsh dioceses including the case for David's official recognition as a Saint. As soon as he returned to Rome, Pope Callistus issued to Bishop Bernard a Papal Bull from the Lateran Palace in which he associated David's name with that of Saint Andrew, the Apostle and Patron of his original monastery, as the Patron Saints of St David's. In effect, this recognised Saint David's cult that thus progressed from being local to become national, and crossed the Welsh borders to be accepted in the Province of Canterbury.

As time went by David attracted many admiring followers among the Anglican Communion, one of whom was the clergyman and hymn writer Sabine Baring-Gould who said that 'Dewi is still the one purely Welsh Saint whom Pope Callistus II has formally enrolled in the calendars of the Western Church.' Later, Pope Alexander III, 1159-1181, re-affirmed that canonisation was the prerogative of the Roman See, though some bishops retained their right of local beatification. Matters were finally resolved in 1234 by Pope Gregory IX, the friend and supporter of Saint Dominic and Saint Francis, who decreed that only Papal Canonisation was legitimate.

Once Pope Callistus had published his Papal Bull, no time was lost in ensuring that liturgical commemorations of Saint David were included in the Welsh, Irish, and Scottish Martyrologies, and those of England at Canterbury, Exeter and Sarum. They also appeared in most monastic and diocesan calendars, litanies, breviaries and missals and, given Saint Andrew's association, it is understandable that there should be prominent insertions in the Aberdeen Breviary. At the same time, attention was given to the composition of the music for the Office of Saint David's Feast on 1st March. A significant liturgical text in a manuscript in the Library of Hereford Cathedral includes the Proper of the Mass for Saint David that is graced with the Collect:

> O God, who didst foretell Thy blessed Confes-
> sor and Pontiff David by the message of an
> angel to Saint Patrick thirty years before his
> birth, we beseech Thee that, by his intercession
> whose memory we celebrate, we may come to
> eternal joys.

Prior to the Gospel, there is also a beautiful Sequence
that begins 'David, star of heavenly splendour'. Saint
David's commemoration on 1st March, now a Solemnity in Wales and a Feast in England, begins with the
Prayer

> Grant, Almighty God, that we may be protected
> by the loving intercession
> of your blessed confessor bishop David,
> and that we who keep his feast
> may also imitate his firmness in defending the
> Catholic Faith;
> through Our Lord Jesus Christ your Son
> who lives and reigns with you
> and the Holy Spirit, One God for ever and ever.
> Amen.

Miracle and legend

The early Saints were properly revered and admired
for their devotion and zealous promulgation of the
Faith. We learn from their biographers that, even from
childhood, they were blessed with miraculous powers
to help human beings and animals, and to exercise
some control over the elements and the machinations
of the Devil. The details of their lives were so much
part of the religious heritage of the Church that, when
they came to be written down in the eleventh and
subsequent centuries, their saintly activities appeared
as fresh in the minds of the writers as if they had

witnessed the events. Admittedly, the competitive spirit among mediaeval biographers sometimes led to over-statement or embellishments that were difficult either to prove or contradict. In such circumstances we may exercise a willing and child-like suspension of disbelief, just as one can apply critical judgment while accepting that, as in the Scriptures, well-disposed and pious imagination has its place in circumstances that God makes holy for our benefit.

Rhygyfarch's account of the miracle attending David's Baptism has been mentioned earlier. Another interesting legend involves the Irish Abbot-Bishop Saint Finbarr, 560–610, who is Patron of Cork and Barra in the Outer Hebrides where he founded famous and influential monasteries. On his way home from a pilgrimage to Rome, he stopped in Wales to greet his old friend David.

> When the time came for him to return to his monks in Ireland, he was disappointed to find there was no wind to fill the sails of his ship, so he asked for the horse on which the holy David had been wont to ride. Having obtained David's blessing, and putting his trust in David and the support of his horse, he used it for a ship inasmuch as the horse ploughed through the swelling waves as if through a level field. Nearing the shores of Ireland, he caught sight of Saint Brendan who was leading a wondrous life on a marine animal. When Saint Brendan saw a man horse-riding in the sea he exclaimed 'God is wonderful in His Saints.' The horseman drew near to where he was so that they were able to exchange greetings. When he arrived in Ireland, Saint Finbarr told his monks the wonderful story and showed them David's horse

that stayed in the service of the monastery until it died. In memory of the miracle, they painted the horse's image that may still be found in Ireland covered in gold and renowned for the number of its miracles.[1]

Saint Brendan 'the Navigator', 486-575, was Abbot of Clonfert and, like many Celtic monks was a great traveller whose missions took him to Scotland, Brittany and Wales where he was, for a time Abbott of Llancarvan. His popular cult owed much to the 'Navigation of Saint Brendan', a visionary romance written by an Irish monk in the ninth century that transformed the historical, seafaring Abbot into a mythical adventurer who accomplished incredible exploits. These have been celebrated by Matthew Arnold in his poem 'Saint Brandan'.

If the Irish owe the absence of snakes to Saint Patrick, it seems they can be grateful to Saint David for the beneficent presence of their bees! The story goes that Saint and Abbot Modomnoc of Leinster, who was of the royal O'Neil family of Ireland, had been one of David's theology students in Menevia. While he was there, one of his responsibilities was to look after the bees but, when the time came for him to return to Ireland, the swarm that had grown to love him settled on the ship's prow. He did not wish to deprive the monastery of its bees so he turned back with them. They followed but would not leave him, and this happened several times until eventually David gave him permission to take them with him. David blessed them and said, 'May the land to which you hasten abound with your offspring. Never may your progeny be wanting, but never again shall your offspring grow up in our monastery.'[2] Rhygyfarch could not resist adding

> We have learnt by experience that this still continues, for we find swarms that go into the monastery of Father David remain only a little while and gradually cease. Ireland, however, wherein bees could never before exist, is enriched with an abundance of honey. And so, by the blessing of the holy Father David they have multiplied in Ireland. These and many other things did the holy Father David do.
>
> We have collected these few things which have been found scattered in very old writings of the country, especially at Menevia itself, which have survived till now, eaten away by the constant devouring of moths and the ravages of the years through the hours and seasons, and written according to the old style of the ancients.[3]

Notes

[1]   Rhygyfarch, *Life of St David*, 39–40.

[2]   See *ibid.*, 43.

[3]   *Ibid.*, 43, 66.

7

Devotion to Saint David

Saint David in Art, Poetry and Music

David is described by Gerald of Wales as tall and physically strong, with a benign, serene countenance. He is usually depicted as a bishop in episcopal vestments and mitre, and holding a crozier, He stands on a mound of earth as a gold-beaked dove whispers in his ear, an allusion to his dramatic and eloquent appearance at the Synod of Brevi. David's popularity in Wales is evident in the poem 'Armes Prydein Vawr' in which the poet prophesied that when all would seem lost, the people would unite to follow David as their leader, 'and they will raise his banner and defeat the English.'

The music for the Office of the Feast, composed when Pope Callistus II officially recognised Saint David's sanctity in 1119, was edited in 1990 by O. T. Edwards in *Matins, Lauds and Vespers for Saint David's Day: the mediaeval Office of the Welsh Patron Saint*.[1] The modern composers Arwel Hughes and Karl Jenkins wrote further choral works that reflect David's life and the themes of his final sermon.

The National Emblem of Wales

The fact that the leek may have been a frugal item in the diet of David's monks may account for its being considered an emblem of Wales. In Shakespeare's *Henry V*, the Welsh Captain Fluellen reminds the King that 'Welshmen did good service in a garden where leeks did grow, wearing leeks in their Monmouth caps which, your majesty know, to this hour is an honourable badge of the service; and I do believe your majesty takes no scorn to wear the leek upon Saint Tavy's day,' and Henry agrees, 'I wear it for a memorable honour.' Fluellen may have also had in mind the legend that the leek was worn on Saint David's Day 'in memory of a victorious battle against Saxon invaders when, on the Saint's advice, the Welsh wore leeks in their caps to distinguish them from their enemies.' Later Fluellen has an altercation with the English 'counterfeit, cowardly knave' Ancient ('Ensign') Pistol. Even though provoked, it was rather unkind of him to force the hapless, lowly infantry officer to eat a raw leek. Nowadays, many of Saint David's compatriots find wearing the daffodil, 'Cennyn Pedr', more congenial and convenient. David's Welsh name 'Dafydd' explains Fluellen's 'Saint Tavy', and the further corruption 'Taffy' accounts for the colloquialism for any Welsh male. Perhaps we can also thank Saint David for naming the River Taff that flows through Glamorgan to Cardiff and the Bristol Channel.[2]

Pilgrimage to Saint David's Shrine and Cathedral

St David's, the spot David chose for his monastery, is Britain's oldest cathedral settlement. From the sixth century, it survived the ravages of Norse and other invaders, though it was never entirely immune from piratical assaults. After Pope Callistus II had given his blessing to David's cult as a Saint, he enriched St David's as a pilgrim shrine with Indulgences, and declared that two pilgrimages to this place were the equivalent of one to Rome, and three to a pilgrimage to Jerusalem and the Holy Land. This was a great consolation to those who, for reasons of work, finance, health or age, could not undertake long journeys. It became one of Mediaeval Christendom's major shrines, and the road by which it was reached was called *The Holy Way*. It proved an added incentive that David was one of the first identifiable figures in Welsh history and a native of the land of which he is Patron. Royal pilgrims to the Shrine include William the Conqueror; Henry II, still repenting for instigating the murder of Saint Thomas Becket, who took opportunities as he travelled to and from Ireland on affairs of state; Edward I and his Queen Eleanor who presented memorial velvet copes to the Sacristy; and our reigning Monarch, Queen Elizabeth II who, while at St David's, raised it to the status of a city albeit the smallest in her kingdom.

The present cruciform Cathedral of 1176 has a beautiful nave where centuries of craftsmanship present a scene of mediaeval splendour. The roof and choir stalls express the carver's skill not least on the hinged seats with their *misericord* rests that depict the sense of humour that can accompany piety.[3] Among the impressive effigies of previous Bishops and Welsh nobility are those of Bishop Henry Gower, 1328-4, who is remembered for refurbishing and extending buildings including the Bishop's Palace. Then, at the High Altar, lies Edmund Tudor, Earl of Richmond and father of Henry VII who founded the Welsh-Tudor dynasty.[4] An interior wall houses the 'Abraham Stone' which is an example of the Celtic art that once adorned the graves of the sons of Bishop Abraham who was killed during a Viking raid in 1080.

In the nineteenth century, some the need for urgent restoration work was recognised and initiated, inspired by the ethos of the Oxford Movement of the Anglican Communion. This sought and advocated spiritual, doctrinal and liturgical renewal through a return to the teaching of the Church Fathers, and promoting the universal Catholic Church as a divinely authorised institution, sought visible unity through the Sacraments and the unbroken apostolic succession of bishops. Its acknowledged leader was John Henry Newman, later a convert to Catholicism, a Cardinal, and beatified by Pope Benedict XVI in September 2010.

During the restoration work, directed by the architect Sir Gilbert Scott, the bones of a tall man and another of less height were discovered. It is believed these are the remains of Saint David himself and his friend Saint Justinian who had lived a solitary life of prayer on Ramsey Island off the Pembroke coast before dying a martyr's death at the hands of pagan invaders. They are both now at rest in the Holy Trinity Chapel where David's life is portrayed in mosaics that are visited by Christians of all denominations, members of other faiths, and those of none.

The Well of David's mother Saint Non returned to Catholic hands in 1934 when Bishop Francis Vaughan of Menevia laid the foundation stone of a Catholic chapel that was erected over the Well, so the Mass that David loved is once more celebrated in this outpost of the Faith.

The Most Reverend Francis Mostyn who from 1921 to 1939 was the fourth Archbishop of Cardiff wrote a stirring hymn in Saint David's honour for which the beautiful melody 'St David' was written by Dom Anthony Gregory Murray OSB, monk of Downside.

O Great Saint David, still we hear thee call us
Unto a life that knows no fear of death;
Yea down the ages will thy words enthral us,
Strong happy words: 'Be joyful, keep the Faith.'
On Cambria's sons stretch out thy hands in blessing,
For our dear land thy help we now implore.
Lead us to God, with humble hearts confessing
Jesus, Lord and King for evermore.

Christ was the centre rock of all thy teaching,
God's holy will—the splendour of its theme,
His grace informed, His love inflamed thy preaching;
Christ's sway on earth, the substance of thy dream.
Refrain: On Cambria's sons...

In early childhood, choosing Jesus only,
Thy fervour showed his yoke was light and sweet;
And thus for thee, life's journey was not lonely—
The path made plain by prints of wounded feet.
Refrain: On Cambria's sons...

O glorious Saint, we wander in the dark;
With thee we seek our trusted guide in Rome,
Help him to steer on earth Saint Peter's barque,
That we may safely reach our heavenly home.
Refrain: On Cambria's sons...

The author and poet E. J. Newell, 1853–1916, wrote a similarly inspiring hymn that celebrates Saint David, and is sung to the melody 'Claudius' adapted from a song by G. W. Fink, 1783-1846.[5]

We praise thy name all holy Lord,
For him, the beacon light
That shone beside our western sea
Through mists of ancient night;
Who sent to Ireland's fainting Church
New tidings of thy word;
For David, prince of Cambrian saints,
We praise thee, holy Lord.

For all the saintly band whose prayers
Still gird our land about,
Of whom, lest men disdain their praise,
The voiceless stones cry out;
Our hills and vales on every hand
Their names and deeds record;
For these, thy ancient hero-host,
We praise thee holy Lord.

Grant us but half their burning zeal,
But half their iron faith,
But half their charity of heart,
And fortitude to death;
That we with them and all thy saints
May in thy truth accord,
And ever in thy holy Church
May praise thee holy Lord.

Notes

[1]   O. T. Edwards, *Matins, Lauds and Vespers for Saint David's Day: the mediaeval Office of the Welsh Patron Saint* (National Library of Wales: 1990).

[2]   See W. Shakespeare, *Henry V*, Act IV Sc vii ll 95ff; Act V Sc i ll 35ff.

3   A *misericord* (sometimes named mercy seat, like the Biblical object) is a small wooden shelf on the underside of a folding seat in a church, installed to provide a degree of comfort for a person who has to stand during long periods of prayer.

4   Cf. W. Shakespeare, *Richard III*.

5   See *Hymns Ancient and Modern*, 575.

Epilogue

Saint David imbued his Welsh children with a profound and abiding Catholicism in the Church built upon the Rock that is Peter, and a loyalty to the Supreme Pontiff who is the Bishop of Rome and the Apostles' successor. Throughout the centuries, it has withstood all the storms and buffetings that have beset it, and even the imposition of a State religion was whole-heartedly resisted in 'Dewi's Land', whose people recalled the voice of David saying, 'Persevere in those things which you have learned from me. Be joyful; keep the Faith.'

The Reformation and after

From the 1520s, Martin Luther and the other Reformers had their disciples and admirers in Britain's universities, coastal towns and cities, but it was the determination of Henry VIII to divorce Catherine of Aragon that gave the Reformation its telling impetus. During Henry VIII's reign Wales became part of the realm of England, and the four Welsh dioceses of St David's, Bangor, Llandaff and St Asaph that had been established in the country under Norman rule, became part of the English Church In 1534, the King separated himself from Rome, declared himself supreme head of the Church in England and set about the dissolution of the monasteries. All the Welsh religious houses were suppressed in 1536 with deep social implications for the people of Wales. Curiously, in company with many bishops and courtiers, he did not entirely reject Catholic doctrine and practice, and even executed some Protestants for heresy, but he martyred Catholics like Saint John Fisher and Saint Thomas More whom he falsely accused of treason and disobedience to the Crown. It was not until the accession of Edward VI in 1547 that Protestantism, led by Thomas Cranmer, Nicholas Ridley and Hugh Latimer, became the 'official' religion in England, and a new liturgy was introduced in 'The Book of Common Prayer'. After a brief resurgence of Catholicism during the rule of Mary from 1553 to 1558, Elizabeth I and her Parliament issued the Acts of Supremacy and Uniformity, and made the episcopal organisation of the Church subservient to the Throne.

Reports made to the Government in England regularly condemned Welsh fidelity to the Catholic Church. In 1569, a Protestant bishop bemoaned the fact that 'the people were not welcoming the new religion and wanted a return to the Romish religion again.' William Barlow, who was unfortunate enough to be chosen as the first Protestant bishop of the historic Catholic diocese of Menevia, did his utmost to suppress 'the Faith of our Fathers'. That he found the task beyond him is summed up in his evaluation that his 'diocese has always been a daughter of Rome.' He was outraged that 'a priest celebrating the Communion Service did, after the Popish manner, break the Host in pieces, and people brought their dead to be buried with songs and candles lighted up.'

An elderly retainer called Elis ap Hywel had, for many years, served as the Cathedral's curator, bell ringer, grave digger, and had undertaken additional responsibility for the churchyard. In 1571, he was summarily dismissed because, 'he being sexton in the cathedral Church of St David had, for a long time, been hiding and preserving ungodly Popish books in the hope of better days to come'. Further dismay was expressed 'in that the people of Carmarthen do kneel and knock their breasts at the sight of the Communion', and that 'when the local reforming bishop ordered a Catholic altar to be transferred to the middle of the church and used as a mere Communion table, it caused such an outcry among the people that he had to restore it to its rightful position without delay.' As late as 1722, Erasmus Saunders, writing about attitudes prevailing in St David's explained, 'If we have not quite abandoned the errors of our Popish ancestors, it is because the doctrines of the Reformation begun two hundred years ago in England have not effectually reached us.' Perhaps a little more forthright was a reaction noticed by a Spanish Ambassador who wrote to his King: 'the Welsh counties tell the Earl of Pembroke not to send any preachers across the marches in case they do not return alive'!

The Welsh Martyrs

The Forty Martyrs of England and Wales whose Feast is now celebrated on 4th May, gave their lives in supreme witness to the truth of Catholic belief and teaching, and their tradition is one in which all have shared and from which all may draw strength across ecumenical boundaries. They were put to death on the specious grounds of various supposed transgressions. First, there were the alleged contraventions of the Treason Act that had been passed in 1352 by Edward III that forbade plotting against the King or his heirs. Then use was made of Elizabeth's Act by which she demanded obedience from all her subjects, and condemned as treasonable any attempt to reconcile others, or being reconciled, to the Catholic Church, that is 'persuading to Popery with seditious words against the Queen'. The third opportunity arose from an additional Act that outlawed 'the Jesuits, priests, and such other disobedient persons.' After 1559, if a priest who had been ordained abroad, had entered or remained in the realm was captured, he would be condemned to death for treason, and the same fate awaited anyone who to helped or sheltered him.

Of these Martyrs, seven were Welsh. Saint Richard Gwyn, the first to suffer in the reign of Elizabeth, was born in 1537 at Llanidloes, Montgomeryshire and studied at Oxford and Cambridge before returning to Wales in 1562. He and his wife were renowned for their devotion to marriage and family life that was blessed by six children, and he taught in Flintshire and Denbyshire schools before being condemned to death at Wrexham in 1584. Saint John Jones was born at Clynnog Fawr near Caernarvon in 1559 and became a Franciscan whom Pope Clement VIII described as 'a true religious of Saint Francis.' His apostolate was in the London area before arrest and imprisonment in The Clink, and he was martyred in Southwark in 1598. Saint John Roberts, originally from Monmouth, was a scholar of St John's College, Oxford. While still a young man, he was converted to Catholicism and studied for the priesthood at Valladolid. After his ordination, he entered the Order of Saint Benedict and served the Benedictine mission in London until he gave his life for the Faith at Tyburn in 1610.

Four of the seven fell victim to the anti-Catholic persecution initiated by the infamous Titus Oates who, in 1678, concocted the story that the Jesuits were plotting to kill the English king Charles II.

Saint John Kemble, born in 1599 at St Weonards near Welsh Newton, studied for the Priesthood at Douai where he was ordained in 1625. He returned to Monmouth and served as an itinerant pastor for half a century, winning many admirers even among non-Catholics. His apparently secure base at Pembridge Castle that his brother had leased in 1630 did not protect him from arrest and sentence of death. Despite the fact that his nephew Richard had saved Charles's life at the battle of Worcester, the King made no grateful effort to intervene. John, now eighty, was condemned in Hereford as a Priest, taken to London to be interrogated by Oates, and sent back to Hereford for execution on 22nd August 1679. On the scaffold he asked for time to say his prayers, smoke a last pipe and have a glass of sack, and forgave his executioner. His severed hand is still a treasured relic in the church of Saint Francis Xavier in Hereford.

Saint David Lewis was born in Abergavenny in 1616 and, after ordination in Rome in 1642, joined the Jesuits. Based at Cwm, he was a missionary in South Wales for thirty-six years before his arrest in Monmouthshire and being taken to London with John Kemble. He was returned to Usk where he was hanged, drawn and quartered on August 27th 1679. Saint Philip Evans, born in Monmouth in 1645, joined the Jesuits at St Omer in 1665 and, after ordination to the priesthood in Liege ten years later, returned as a missionary to South Wales. Saint John Lloyd from Brecon, studied for the priesthood at Valladolid in 1653 and served the Welsh mission valiantly for twenty-four years. After capture and condemnation, they were cell-mates in Cardiff Castle where they were martyred together on 22nd July 1679.

The continuing Welsh Mission

Continued persecution of Catholics in Wales, and the effect of the Penal Laws, imposing heavy fines and imprisonment for failing to attend Protestant church services, slowly but surely reduced the Catholic presence in the country. The Church relied on missioners from abroad to maintain its Sacramental life, and these priests became scarcer and scarcer—often to be found on the estates of influential Catholic families, who could hide and protect them.

From 1688 the Holy See appointed vicars apostolic to care for the Church in Britain, and Wales became part of the Western District, administered by a succession of Benedictines and Franciscans. The penal laws were gradually eased from the end of the eighteenth century, culminating in 1829 with the Catholic Emancipation Act when a great many—but by no means all—restrictions on Catholics were removed. In 1840 the Western District was divided in two, with Herefordshire, Monmouthshire and Wales becoming the Welsh District with its own vicar apostolic, the Benedictine Bishop Brown. Then, in 1850, the diocese of Newport and Menevia was created as a suffragan see of Westminster. Only in 1916 was the Cardiff Province established, consisting of the Metropolitan Archdiocese of Cardiff with the diocese of Menevia as a suffragan see, with the Benedictine James Bilsborrow as the first Archbishop. Today the Province is divided into three dioceses—Cardiff, Menevia and Wrexham.

In penal times, the Faith was sustained in great measure by missioners from abroad, and the priests like Saint John Roberts are a reminder that, since the days of Saint David, the Benedictine Order has been at the forefront of the Welsh Mission which even the Dissolution of the Monasteries failed to stifle. In his person, David Augustine Baker (the Benedictine mystic Dom Augustine Baker), an Abergavenny man born in 1575, provides a link between the pre-Reformation monks of Westminster Abbey and the continued Benedictine presence in Britain.

Herefordshire, rich with Celtic monastic activity in St David's time, continues today as a part of the Welsh Province of the Church. Here the Benedictine presence in the Catholic Church of Wales is based—until 1916, the Abbey Church of St Michael the Archangel at Belmont was the pro-cathedral for the diocese of Newport and Menevia, and then, for four years the cathedral of the Archdiocese of Cardiff. Its monks have served parishes across South Wales.

Just as the Celtic monks risked life and limb in the cause of Evangelism, so the Holy Spirit inspired their successors to recognize opportunities to preach the Gospel to good effect. The mediaeval Cistercian followers of Saint Benedict's Rule had founded abbeys throughout Wales in Margam, Neath, Whitland, Abbeys Cymmer and Dore, Valle Crucis, Basingwerk, Cwmhir, and Saint Dogmell's, after the revered sixth-century Welsh monk. Though these have disappeared with the passing of time, their beneficent influence survives in places like the present Parish of the Holy Cross Abbey in Whitland, Camarthenshire. In 1913, the Order established the Abbey of Our Lady and Saint Samson on Caldey Island off Tenby and also celebrates Mass on the site of the sixth century church that was dedicated to Saint David.

Catholic worship never ceased in Abergavenny during the penal years, and in 1687, nearly a century after the martyrdom of Saint John Jones and shortly after Saint John Wall's equally noble sacrifice, their Franciscan brethren opened the mission of Our Lady and Saint Michael in Abergavenny, now a Benedictine Priory currently served by the monks of Belmont Abbey. The Capuchins have cared for the Pontypool Parish of Saint Alban since 1884. The Society of Jesus continues to minister to Welsh Catholics in the Carmarthenshire Parishes of Ammanford, Newcastle Emlyn, and Burry Port.

The Benedictine and Franciscan missioners were joined by the Rosminian priests of the Institute of Charity with their associated teaching Sisters of Providence, the Sisters of Nazareth, the Daughters of Charity of Saint Vincent de Paul, the Daughters of the Holy Spirit, the Poor Clares, and the Sisters of Saint Joseph. Also, to David's See of Menevia, came the Cistercians, Jesuits, Carmelites, the Irish Union of Ursulines and the Daughters of Charity, though this list does not pretend to be exhaustive.

The first half of the eighteenth century was an unhappy time in France where the reigns of Louis XIV and Louis XV witnessed secular and clerical efforts to release the Church from Roman control with unprofitable results. Lavish expenditure in high places and unlimited privileges for the affluent led to the people's insupportable taxation and consequent desperation. In contrast to royal and aristocratic self-satisfaction, they were miserable, felt excluded from any say in government, resentful of inequality, and increasingly rebellious.

When Pope Pius VI was elected in 1775, he was immediately confronted by growing nationalism, secularism and atheism that aroused tension between Church and State which Louis XVI proved unable to resolve. The deteriorating situation and a beleaguered populace resulted in the eruption of the French Revolution in 1789 that introduced a reign of Terror lasting two years during which the Revolutionaries adopted an anti-clerical programme that included the closure of churches unless they were served by clergy who swore allegiance to a State Church. Priests who refused to submit, went into hiding, were deported or executed, and members of Religious Orders either disguised themselves or left for other European countries to demonstrate that the practice of the Faith and fidelity to the Church was associated with persevering heroism. French priests and religious, exiled by successive waves of anti-clerical legislation, made important contributions to the development of the pastoral and spiritual life of the Church both in England and in Wales in the nineteenth and twentieth centuries.

The Potato Famine from 1845 to 1849 caused untold suffering in Ireland and great family sadness. Many found it necessary to migrate, especially to Wales where the Church was already benefiting from the Irish missionary spirit, and which now received an added impetus from the new arrivals. From the middle of the nineteenth century, cities and towns like Cardiff,

Newport and beyond were blessed by the arrival of families who were courageously dedicated to the Faith.

Many noble diocesan priests left their native land to cross the sea for the salvation of souls, and Institutes like the Brothers of the Christian Schools arrived to build and teach in schools. Devout family life ensured a steady supply of vocations to the priesthood and religious life, and Catholic parents also nurtured the children who became the dedicated professionals who, at no small sacrifice, undertook training to teach in the parish schools. These were attached to the churches that appeared almost miraculously from the 1840's thanks to the selfless trust and commitment of the clergy, and the laity's generosity that was so admirable in harsh circumstances. Early examples include The Metropolitan Cathedral of Saint David in Cardiff that dates from 1842; St Illtyd's, Dowlais, 1844; St Dyfrig's, Treforest, 1857; St Peter's, Cardiff, 1861; Our Lady of the Angels, Cwmbran, 1864; St Patrick's, Grangetown, 1866; St David's and St Patricks, Haverfordwest, 1872; St Alban's, Cardiff, 1891.

Through all challenges throughout the centuries since Saint David's time, the Catholic Faith has adorned Welsh history. That the Celts have long memories to accompany their deep devotion was understood by G. K. Chesterton who said of Saint David:

Mine eyes were shy with secrets;
A hymn is hid in my speech;
it may cry to Thee still.

Chesterton also wrote a poem for St David's Day:

My eyes are void with vision; I sing but I cannot speak;
I hide in the vaporous caverns like a creature wild and weak;

But for ever my harps are tuned and for ever my songs are sung,
And I answer my tyrants ever in an unknown tongue.

Doubtless, the Patron Saint would wish us all to conclude with A Prayer for Wales:

Almighty God who in Your infinite goodness
have sent Your only-begotten Son into this world
to open once more the gates of Heaven
and to teach us how to know, love and serve You,
have mercy on Your people who dwell in Wales.
Grant to them the precious gift of Faith
and unite them to the one, true Church
founded by Your Divine Son;
that acknowledging her authority and obeying her voice,
they may serve You, love You and worship You
as You desire in this world,
and obtain for themselves everlasting happiness
in the world to come.
Through the same Christ our Lord. Amen.

Our Lady, Help of Christians, pray for Wales.
Saint David, pray for Wales.
Saint Winefride, pray for Wales.

Acknowledgements

Grateful acknowledgement is made for recourse to the following works.

Attwater, D., *The Penguin Dictionary of Saints*. London: 1972.

Butler, A., *The Lives Of The Fathers, Martyrs, And Other Principal Saints*. London: Virtue and Co. Ltd., 1926.

Chadwick, O., *History of Christianity*. London: Weidenfeld and Nicolson, 1995.

Cowles, F. I., *Pilgrim Ways*. London: Burns, Oates & Washbourne, 1934.

Crowley, D., *St David of Wales*. London: CTS, 1953.

Deansley, M., *A History of the Medieval Church*. London, Methuen, 1951.

Farmer, D. H., *Oxford Dictionary of Saints*. Oxford: OUP, 1978.

Knowles OSB, D., *Christian Monasticism*. London: Weidenfeld & Nicolson, 1969.

Midgley, J. B., *Benedict, Patron of Europe*. London: CTS, 2005.

Page, R. I., *Life in Anglo-Saxon England*. Batsford, London 1970.

Savage, A. (tr.), *The Anglo-Saxon Chronicles*. London: Greenwich Editions, 2002.

Wade, A. W., *The Life of Saint David*. London: SPCK, 1923.

Walsh, J., *Forty Martyrs of England and Wales*. London: CTS, 1972.

Ward, H., & Wild, J., *Christian Quotation Collection*. London: Lion Publishing, 1997.

Wyn Evans J. & Wooding, J. M., *St David of Wales*. Woodbridge: Boydell Press, 2007.

Encyclopaedia of Catholicism, New York: Harper and Collins, 1995.

Catholic Encyclopaedia. London: The Encyclopaedia Press, 1907.

The Jerusalem Bible. London: Darton, Longman & Todd, 1974.

The Daily Missal, London: Collins, 1982.

The Roman Missal, London: Burns, Oates & Washbourne, 1948.

The Westminster Hymnal. London: Burns, Oates & Washbourne, 1939.

Hymns Ancient and Modern. London: William Clowes & Sons, 1930.

Lightning Source UK Ltd.
Milton Keynes UK
UKOW050240180212

187502UK00001B/71/P